Eric Audinet

Visiting the Island of Ré

Photographs by the Author

Translation by Angela Moyon

ÉDITIONS SUD OUEST

For Caroline

Ré, which only just emerges above sealevel, has not really been an island since the inauguration of the bridge linking the Pointe de Sablanceaux and La Rochelle in 1988. Yet it is vital to ensure that this outstanding feature of the Atlantic Coast remains unspoilt and keeps its character and charm.

The island stretches over a distance of 25 km (16 miles) from east to west, from the easterly headland called Pointe de Sablanceaux to the Phare des Baleines, the lighthouse looking out towards the Americas. It lies only 9 km (6 miles) from La Rochelle and less than 4 km (3 miles) from the breakwater at La Pallice, jutting out into the Atlantic Ocean between the straits known as the Pertuis Breton to the north and the Pertuis d'Antioche to the south.

Almost the entire island is covered by sand dunes planted with pines and tamarisk. Where the rock does push through to the surface, there is Mediterranean-style scrub with sea-campion, myrtle and rosemary. Around the shores of the island, the Jurassic rock extends into shallows draped with seaweed.

The Island of Ré is very flat. It consists of three tiny islets which man has linked together over the centuries. To the east, and now connected to the mainland by the bridge, is Saint-Martin, the island of fields. To the west is Ars, linked to its neighbour by the Martray isthmus; this is the island of salt-pans around Le Fier d'Ars. Finally, to the north between the other two lies l'Oye (or Loix) which is linked to Saint-Martin by a narrow road that twists and turns across the marshes.

You will no longer see donkeys dressed in striped trousers working in the fields, nor women wearing the island head-dress, but the Island of Ré has nevertheless retained many of its traditions, the most important being the quality of the landscape, passing from wild moorland to salt-marshes, from woods and meadows to the mudflats of the Le Fier area. This is an outstanding natural environment, with a fragile balance that must be maintained.

A town of contrasts with its hard labour camp and, at the same time, its delightful yachting marina. Saint-Martin is the main town on the island, a popular venue for holidaymakers in the summer months. (Photo by André Barathieu).

The Island of Ré bridge links La Rochelle to the Pointe de Sablanceaux.

The flower-decked dykes in Loix, beyond the salt-pans.

Overleaf : The harbour in Saint-Martin has two main basins, one for pleasure craft, the other for fishing boats.

TOURING THE ILSLAND

Over the bridge to Ré

Nowadays, the island is linked to the mainland by a huge bridge 2.9 km (2 miles) long stretching in a curve from La Rochelle to Sablanceaux and rising some 30 metres (37 ft.) above the highest tides. The roadway is 15.50 metres (50 ft.) wide and is supported on 28 pillars 5.50 metres (18 ft.) in diameter resting on the foundations in the seabed. Visitors scarcely have time to accustom themselves to the sea air before they begin the dizzying descent onto the island, with the breakwater and huge boats at La Pallice on their left and a misty view over the the villages of Rivedoux, La Flotte, Sainte-Marie and Saint-Martin jutting up from a flat landscape only just visible between the straits. On each side of the bridge are the pontoons at Sablanceaux, now deserted except by seagulls.

The tiny harbour in La Flotte, one of the oldest on the island, facing out onto the Pertuis Breton.

From Sablanceaux to Rivedoux where light takes on a new meaning

Visitors arriving on this tongue of land that, for many years, bristled with forts and other military buildings because it was the closest landing point to the mainland, are immediately struck by the change of air - and the difference in the light. The sand is golden yellow. Behind the pine trees and tamarisks are the seemingly endless beach and blue, blue sea.

The tree-lined road quickly reaches Rivedoux, the first village on the island. To the left is a row of small whitewashed cottages with green shutters, their walls covered in hollyhocks in the summer months. To the right is the harbour with its jetty and brightly-coloured fishing boats. Although tourism is a major source of income here, it is oyster farming with its beds laid out in the cove at Rivedoux which provides most of the economic wealth. In the village, the road splits in two. One road runs down to Sainte-Marie and the south coast; the other continues to La Flotte on the north coast, after running through a small area of woodland.

LR 579 307

LR316 192

Fort de la Prée, the oldest fortress on the island

Almost 3 km (2 miles) from Rivedoux stands Fort de la Prée. Built in the 1620's to strengthen the island's defences, this star-shaped construction is the oldest fortress on the island. It played a major role in the English invasion of 1627 when it acted as a relay between Saint-Martin and the mainland.

Abbaye des Châteliers and its eventful history

This extraordinary building, or to be more precise what remains of it, stands further on, in the middle of fields on the clifftops overlooking the sea. From the road, these majestic ruins are an impressive sight.

History did not spare the Abbey of Our Lady of Ré, better known as Notre-Dame des Châteliers. It was founded by Cistercians in the mid 12th Century and attacked twice by the English. It was rebuilt on each occasion but again pillaged and set alight by Protestants in 1574 and 1623. After that, the monks decided to abandon it to its fate.

Almost nothing remains of the original church. In the 14th Century, the building was more than 40 metres (130 ft.) long. It had a single aisle and a vast window in the east end. The most admirable features of the ruins are the window frames and the decoration on the capitals. Archaeological digs have revealed the remains of the abbey buildings around the church.

Beyond the fields on the seaward side is a sheer cliff dropping down to the rocky beach below and providing a magnificent view of the Pertuis Breton.

La Flotte-en-Ré and its maze of streets

The tiny harbour in La Flotte, nestling at the head of a cove, is one of the oldest anchorages on the island. In fine weather, the first thing to strike visitors is the extraordinary blend of colours in the sails of the fishing boats, the small green-painted lighthouse at the harbour mouth, the red or blue pullovers of the older locals and the tall whitewashed houses with their vividly-coloured shutters flanking the main square.

Behind the harbour is a maze of narrow streets well sheltered from the wind, a wonderful place for a stroll. The old market is a sight not to be missed, as is the parish church dedicated to St. Catherine. It was built in the 14th Century, badly damaged during the Wars of Religion and restored in the early 19th Century after being used as a Temple of Reason during the French Revolution. In the wall running along the street is a superb Gothic doorway. Nearby, concealed behind high walls, is the magnificent residence known as Les Glandiers, which was built *c.* 1695. It has an old well, a dovecote and statues from the reign of Louis XIV.

The road known as Cours Félix Faure runs along the beautiful beach at La Clavette. Further on, wide meadows run gently down to the sea. From here to the beach at La Cible, the rocky foreshore is covered with oyster beds.

Saint-Martin-en-Ré, a town with a glorious past

This is the main town on the island, a fact which is obvious from the superb fortifications, impressive citadel and eventful history. It was a market town in the 12th Century and continued to amass wealth in later times despite various trials and tribulations (including the famous siege of 1627 when Monsieur de Toiras defeated the English) before becoming a magnificent military stronghold thanks to Vauban's constructions. In the following century, it acquired a number of truly splendid buildings. In the 19th Century, successive crises in the salt and wine trades not to mention the introduction of steamships took the town's economy into decline. Not until the last ten years has there been a noticeable improvement.

Entrance to Saint-Martin is by way of a breach in the town walls. On the right are the walls and the Toiras Gate at the end of a stone bridge over a moat, where a few horses now graze. Beyond the breach are the high walls of the prison and the citadel which had a number of famous prisoners in its day, among them Mirabeau, Dreyfus and Papillon.

A road northwards leads to the former naval base. It was here that boats offloaded prisoners sentenced to hard labour who were then taken to New Caledonia or French Guiana.

Turning back towards Saint-Martin, the road arrives at the delightful Parc de La Barbette with its magnificent trees and tiny red and white lighthouse. In fine weather, there is a splendid view right across the Pertuis Breton and along the Vendée coast.

Then come the quaysides. The present harbour dates from the 16th Cen-

Between Rivedoux and La Flotte are the grandiose ruins of the Abbaye des Châteliers which was founded by Cistercian monks in the middle of the 12th Century.

tury but has late 17th-century developments designed by Vauban. It includes two main basins, one for fishing boats and the other a yachting marina. Crowds gather round the fishermen as they land their catches of fish and shrimps; tourists stop at the pavement cafés for a drink. The charming Pierre-Lanier District between the two basins in the harbour has some luxurious residences. It stands like a tiny islet, encircled by yachts and fishing smacks. The Hôtel de Clerjotte, a superb 15th-century mansion which was used as an armaments depot from 1690 onwards, stands on Avenue Boutillier and is now the home of the Naval Museum. It also houses the collections from the former Ernest-Cognacq Museum.

Narrow streets climb up through the old town with its mediaeval houses, its 17th-century squares, the mansion known as the Hôtel des Cadets Gentilshommes, the St. Honoré hospital containing some wonderful exhibits in its museum, and the parish church dedicated to St. Martin at the end of Rue Sully. The church bears witness to the town's eventful past, having been devastated twice by Protestants, partially demolished by Toiras in order to prevent the English from using it as a base, and again damaged by an Anglo-Dutch bombardment in 1696. The beauty of the building as it stands today suggests the extraordinary Gothic style that it must have had in the 15th Century.

The Porte des Campani, a gate named after soldiers in the Champagne regiment who were stationed here in the 17th Century, leads out of Saint-Martin into the heart of the countryside. From there, the road runs to La Couarde.

The curving lines of the bridge seen from Rivedoux.

The church dedicated to St. Catherine in La Flotte-en-Ré. Built in the 14th Century, it was destroyed during the Wars of Religion and used as a Temple of Reason during the French Revolution.

The yachting marina in Ars en Ré, the most westerly harbour on the island overlooking the vast expanse of Fier.

La Couarde-sur-Mer, the hollyhock village

This village lies at the junction of the two main roads running across the eastern side of the island, the north road through La Flotte and Saint-Martin and the south road through Le Bois and Sainte-Marie. From here, there is only one road to Le Fiers d'Ars. The main source of income for La Couarde is now wine-growing but the village also has a wonderful beach which attracts crowds of tourists in the summer (La Pergola is a favourite meeting-place for all the island's young people). This is a village filled with hollyhocks and wisteria at the right season, a delightful place for a gentle stroll.

The Loix peninsula and the salt-pans

Just at the edge of the Henri IV woods, at La Passe, a narrow road leads off to the right, heading northwards. Suddenly, the landscape changes. The scenery is totally different to the remainder of the eastern part of Ré. Marshes stretch as far as the eye can see. At the beginning of the Christian era, they separated the island of Saint-Martin from Loix. A drop in the sea level and long, patient work by the islanders created this area of marshland and dykes, mounds of earth and mudflats, a zone that brought the Island of Ré its wealth for many centuries, thanks to the salt-pans.

To find out more, stop at the *Maison des marais salants* on the roadside just before crossing the peninsula.

For centuries, salt and wine were the two main sources of income for the islanders. It would appear that the salt-pans were created on Ré when monks arrived from Vendée in the 11th Century and decided to render their new lands profitable, in particular in the area in Le Fier d'Ars between Les Portes, Ars, La Couarde and

The salt-pans in Loix are crossed by numerous paths which provide a closer view of migratory birds in spring and autumn.

Loix. The land was reclaimed from the sea and protected by dykes and banks of earth. This system continued to operate until the 19th Century when the marshes reached the peak of their profitability.

The outstanding sunshine and frequent summer breezes quickly ensured high yields. In the 1850's, more than 1,500 hectares of marshland were being used to produce over 30,000 tonnes of salt every year.

The salt-pans have been perfected over the ages. They form a complex pattern of banks of earth, mudflats, fields and channels, through which seawater flows and in which salt is eventually harvested.

In winter, the marshes are flooded to protect the dykes from the effects of rain and heavy frost. March sees the beginning of work to drain, clean, and dry out the land, a long arduous task. By mid-May the marshes have to be ready to begin producing salt again. Slight colouring of the seawater indicates that the first «crop» is ready. A whole series of techniques (graining etc.) involving a vast range of implements (wooden rakes, shovels etc.) are then required in order to complete the work successfully. The period of production stretches from mid-June to the end of September if the atmospheric conditions are right.

In days gone by, the transport, storage and sale of salt took up much of the salt-worker's time. Nowadays, his job finishes once the salt has been piled up. Mechanical diggers then arrive to load the salt onto lorries for transport direct to the cooperative.

The activity in the salt-pans has fallen into a rapid decline and only 70 workers still earn their living there, producing 2,000 tonnes a year.

The village of Loix lies some distance from the main roads across the island and has remained a tranquil spot. It is arguably the place where the insular atmosphere can best be felt. To the south, at the mouth of a tiny harbour marking the end of the world, La Fosse de Loix was often used as an anchorage for boats. On the headland is the Fort du Grouin, a 19th-century battery. This area is famous for its

pink shrimps and oyster farming. The tiny road running westwards along the coast leads to La Lasse, a vast stretch of marshland extending into Le Fier d'Ars.

Le Martray and Le Fier d'Ars, a paradise for birds

Back in La Passe, turn into the road on the right. The tongue of earth narrows more and more until, finally, it reaches Le Martray, the narrowest point on the island (60 metres - 65 yds.) flanked by the Atlantic Ocean and the marshes in Le Fier. A long dyke protects this slender belt of land which has often been flooded over the centuries.

On the right is a checkerboard of marshland stretching as far as the eye can see around the Baie du Fier d'Ars, a vast area of wild scenery in which land and sea combine. This is a paradise for birds.

The Island of Ré lies on a major migration route and, every year, thousands of migratory birds that nest in more northerly climes arrive here for the winter.

The rich environment of marshland and coast provide them with ideal conditions. Sandpipers and godwits fill the beachs at Ars. Turnstones and oystercatchers can be seen in the spring, on the rocky shores at Loix, Les Portes, and the Pointe des Baleines. As to the inland salt-pans, they serve as feeding areas and nesting sites.

In 1988, members of the French society for the protection of birds (the L.P.O.) observed 273 species on the island, especially in the nature reserve at Le Lilleau des Niges on the shores of Le Fier d'Ars. Set up in 1980, the reserve covers an area of 150 hectares of which 55 is former marshland. The area is fully protected, making it an ideal spot for the reproduction of migratory birds.

One of the finest sights on the Island of Ré, though, is the arrival of the brent geese. In November, large numbers of them come to the island where they spend the winter in the marshes and mudflats. Their huge flocks are visible from several miles away and the birds can be observed at leisure in the marshes at Ars or Loix. In 1988, more than 16,000 geese were counted here.

Ars-en-Ré and its belltower

Beyond Le Martray, the strip of land widens out again and the road runs into the small town of Ars, the main community in the island's second administrative district. Jutting up above the marshes and the rooftops is the magnificent black and white steeple that serves as a landmark for boats. After an eventful history and a period of immense wealth, Ars like Saint-Martin fell into a steep decline which has only been reversed over the past few years.

In summer, magnificent yachts tie up opposite the Café du Commerce, an excellent place to stop before exploring the marshes beyond the harbour. Apart from the church, which includes some fine archaeological exhibits, the watch towers on Place Carnot are worthy of attention.

Saint-Clément-des-Baleines and its lighthouse

The road runs westward out of Ars, skirting the beautiful State-owned forest in La Combe-à-l'eau and the long, wild beach behind it for a short distance. Saint-Clément is the most recent village on the island. It includes the five hamlets of Le Chabot, La Tricherie, Le Griveau, Le Godinand and, finally, Le Gillieux, each of them separated by fields and vines.

Further on is the tip of the island and the tall lighthouse known as Phare des Baleines, built *c.* 1850 and rising to a height of almost 60 metres (195 ft.) It is said that, over the centuries, schools of whales have often been beached nearby, hence the name of the lighthouse. There are 320 steps up to the top. In fine weather, the view is magnificent with the sea stretching westwards into infinity and the smaller, original lighthouse just down below. To the east is the entire Island of Ré with its glittering marshes, small whitewashed villages, fields and forests and, even further in the distance, the coast of Vendée and the town of La Rochelle.

The superb cove called Conche des Baleines can be reached on foot from the lighthouse. Fromentin discovered the «end of the world» here and claimed that he had «never seen anything more exotic». Le Lizay forest is a wild, untamed area populated with rabbits and partridge, fig trees and everlasting flowers.

From Les Portes-en-Ré to Trousse-Chemise

Les Portes-en-Ré is the last village on the island, on the northernmost tip. It boasts the remains of a prehistoric settlement. It is a favourite with the island's artists and was home to Louis Suire, the best-known of them all.

Eastwards are the beaches of La

The magnificent steeple on the church in Ars-en-Ré is painted black and white and is used as a landmark by boats.

Overleaf: In winter, the marshland in Le Fier d'Ars is the haunt of large numbers of brent geese.

Loge and La Patache, flanking the small wood called Trousse-Chemise which features in one of Charles Aznavour's songs. From there, right at the end of the island, there is a view of the mouth of Le Fier d'Ars.

Le Bois-Plage-en-Ré - from prehistory to seaside resort

Back in La Couarde, instead of taking the Saint-Martin road, follow the southern route to Le Bois. The interior of the island has a pleasant landscape of fields, thickets and vineyards near Le Morinand, in the heart of the island and near Sainte-Marie.

Le Bois has a large number of prehistoric and Gallo-Roman remains and is now one of the largest seaside resorts on Ré thanks to its many beaches. The farming cooperative is worth a visit for a taste of the wonderful local *pineau* (fortified wine).

La Noue, Sainte-Marie and the legend of the Spanish lady

The old village of Les Grenettes was razed to the ground during the last war. Beyond it is La Noue, which lies within the boundaries of Sainte-Marie (the village was a parish as far back as the 11th Century). Its main sources of income are wine and early vegetables, not forgetting tourism which is enjoying considerable expansion.

Not far away in the sand dunes is the tiny St. Saviour's chapel built on the site of a religious building dating back to the 6th Century. The chapel was commissioned by a Spanish noblewoman who survived a terrible shipwreck.

On the way to Sainte-Marie is a statue of Our Lady of La Morande on a Gothic pedestal. It serves as a reminder of a former monastery. In the village dotted with hollyhocks is a church with an octagonal steeple, on a fine square flanked by whitewashed houses.

In fine weather, the view from the beaches at Sainte-Marie extends as far as the coastline of Oléron, the neighbouring island.

Rivedoux and Sablanceaux, journey's end

The final stage on the tour runs pas the marshes at Le Défens and back to Rivedoux, the small harbour at which the tour began. Wait until nightfall before driving back across the bridge so that you can return to the mainland across an archway of light spanning the ocean.

Fishing boats tied up alongside in the harbour in Saint-Martin.

The steeple on the church in Sainte-Marie on the south side of the island.

THE HISTORY OF THE ISLAND OF RÉ

The early days

The Island of Ré was not always an island; at the beginning of the Quaternary Era, it was linked to the mainland. After the last periods of glaciation, the melting ice caused a rise in the sea level and the Pointe de Sablanceaux at the eastern tip of Ré broke away from the Pointe Saint-Marc in La Pallice. Later, the water level descended, uncovering the marshland subjected to the whims of the tides between the islets of Saint-Martin, Ars, Les Portes and Loix.

By the end of the Quaternary Era, Ré had more or less acquired the landscape visitors see today. Man then set about improving it by exploiting the land periodically uncovered around Le Fier d'Ars.

The first inhabitants

There are no traces of human habitation in the Paleolithic period. However, a few Stone Age remains have been found, in particular the strange Pieu Pierroux grave which was discovered in the 19th Century in the village of Le Bois. More recent digs in the north of the island have revealed large quantities of implements and the remains of food.

Reminders of past eras are more numerous from the Gallo-Roman period onwards. For example, a bronze vase filled with coins bearing the effigies of Roman emperors was found in 1852 in La Flotte. There is a section of Roman road in the south of the island. Le Bois has one of the oldest buildings on the island, the Temple of La Clairaie dedicated to Neptune, thought to have been built in 27 B.C. before being used for Christian worship when Christianity was brought to Ré in the 4th Century. Further on, in Sainte-Marie, there is St. Saviour's Chapel dating from the 6th Century and built on the orders of a mysterious Spanish noblewoman who survived a shipwreck.

During the first ten centuries of the Christian era, the Island of Ré belonged to the Dukes of Aquitaine. Yet little is known about this period. The island was wild and untamed, with a very small population. The eastern part was forested; the western part smothered in marshland. The staple diet of islanders was seafood and game.

Viking invasions

In the circumstances, Ré seemed to be an ideal stronghold and it is hardly surprising that it should have attracted the attention of potential invaders. Throughout the 9th Century, it was devastated by the awesome Vikings who set fire to the ducal castle in Sainte-Marie, pillaged religious buildings and massacred the population. In fact, the terrified locals gradually abandoned the ill-fated island and settled on the mainland instead. This demographic exodus was to have an enormous effect on the later history of Ré.

It was not until 911 A.D. after the signing of a treaty by Charles the Simple and Rollo the Viking chieftain that the end of the nightmare seemed to be in sight.

The policy of the Counts of Poitou leads to recovery

The island was in a desperate state, filled with ruins and abandoned villages. The territory passed to the Counts of Poitou who, as sovereigns of their lands, also had jurisdiction over the sea, providing protection for the straits known as Pertuis Breton and Pertuis d'Antioch with a small fleet of ships. They held the rights to shipwrecks, wrecks at sea and fishing and they were fully aware of the island's strategic value. It was a natural fortress from which to brave the sovereigns of France and, in the 10th Century, they took action against the desertification that placed Ré at the mercy of other invaders.

In order to attract people to the island, it was decided to grant it considerable advantages. This was a particularly cunning strategy and people began to move back to the island. Very soon the grounds of the *Coutume Rétaise* were laid down; they were to be finalised in 1289. An island law was created and a local militia founded. At the same time, personal status, the condition of the land, the legal system, fishing and hunting rights, commercial transactions and the political system all enjoyed a particularly liberal regime.

The recovery was spectacular. The fisheries prospered, maritime trade developed thanks to commerce with La Rochelle and Ré established major links with foreign countries. This provided the island with an easy outlet for its wine and its salt.

Two gates in the 17th-century walls provide an entrance to Saint-Martin. This is the Porte des Campani, named after soldiers in the Champagne regiment.

The harbour in Sainte-Marie with its fine house fronts and pale-coloured shutters.

The small harbour in Rivedoux.

The arrival of the Cistercians

The lords of Mauléon, in particular Eble, established links with the Cistercians of Pontigny with a view to setting up an abbey on Ré. It was this that led, in 1178, to the building of the Abbaye des Châteliers on a clifftop looking out to sea between La Flotte and the tiny harbour of La Prée.

Having obtained large donations from the lords of Mauléon, the monks began land clearance and soil improvement. They taught the islanders how to optimise their vineyards and drain the marshes to create salt-pans. By doing so, they gradually created a race of winegrowers, labourers and salt-pan workers, all of them highly specialised.

In the early 13th Century, Savary de Mauléon who needed money to equip a crusade to the Holy Land gave the islands of Ars, Les Portes and Loix to the abbey in Saint-Michel en l'Herm. The islands were then run by the monks.

The extensive work undertaken was, however, interrupted by conflict with foreign countries. The Abbaye des Châteliers was destroyed four times, twice by the English at the end of the 13th Century and in the 15th, and twice during the Wars of Religion. It was after the ransacking of the abbey by the Protestants in 1623 that the monks, tired of having constantly to rebuild, finally abandoned the island on which they had left such a strong mark.

A long series of attacks by the English

The island's revival would undoubtedly have been much swifter if it had not been the subject of endless conflicts, primarily with the English.

When Henry II Plantagenet mounted the throne of England, the Aunis area was annexed to the English crown through Eleanor, Duchess of Poitou and Aquitaine. Until Aunis returned to the crown of France in 1224, the Island of Ré was the scene of never-ending punitive expeditions launched first by one side then the other. Thereafter the cessation of hostilities was to be short-lived. In 1294, the English returned with warlike intentions. The One Hundred Years' War was to make the situation even worse from 1360 onwards and the island passed back and forward between English and French hands. The years 1372, 1387, 1404, 1457 and 1462 were terrible times indeed for this tiny part of Europe that was so coveted by all.

These years were all the more terrible because, despite its militia, the island remained almost devoid of defences or fortifications, with the notable exception of the church-cum-fortress in Saint-Martin which was built between the 12th and 14th Centuries and which played a major spiritual and military role. During the English siege of 1627, Toiras partly demolished it, fearing that it might be used by the island's attackers.

A typical island house in Sainte-Marie.

BOUCQUINGAM
MN 387931

The salt-pans form a checkerboard around Le Fier d'Ars.

At the end of the Middle Ages, the Island of Ré was, like the entire Aunis area, again in a catastrophic position. Wine production had fallen into a steep decline, the salt marshes were earning only one-third of their peace-time value, the abbeys were demolished, and the region was ravaged by the Black Death. When peace returned at the end of the 15th Century, it took massive solidarity to heal the wounds and give the island's social and economic life back its glitter.

The Wars of Religion

Unfortunately, the calm was to be short-lived and the Island of Ré was soon back in the thick of conflict again. When François I mounted the throne and introduced a number of unpopular measures (in particular the salt tax) to finance his military conquests, the result was a vast movement of popular revolt fed by a new tendency, Protestantism. Ré which had as its neighbour La Rochelle, the town that was to become the main centre of Protestant France, soon had a number of ministers in the south of the island, especially in Saint-Martin and La Flotte where the new religion confronting royal authority rapidly gained hold. In 1545, repression began. Catholics and Protestants fought on the island. Gradually, local conflicts required the intervention of the crown. This marked the beginnings of excessive demands - and sixty years of horror.

The war in 1567 led to the capture of the island by the Protestants from La Rochelle. Blaise de Montluc sent in royal troops by sea from Bordeaux. Guided by the Catholic population of the north of the island, the soldiers landed in Le Fier d'Ars and attacked the famous fortified church in Saint-Martin where the Protestants had sought refuge. Carnage ensued and the Island of Ré returned to the crown of France.

In 1572, the St. Bartholomew's Day massacre ruined any chance of reconciliation. It was followed by the Siege of La Rochelle where many islanders joined their fellow Protestants. After the signing of a treaty, the town immediately sought to take control of the straits and, on 11th March 1574, La Noue captured the island,

An increasingly rare sight: harvesting salt in the marshes.

chased out the Catholic population and destroyed the churches and abbeys. Henri III's reaction was swift. In September 1575, royal troops again landed and entered Saint-Martin, almost without a fight. However, Protestant reinforcements arrived from La Rochelle under cover of darkness and massacred the Catholics while they were asleep.

Until the signature of the Edict of Nantes in 1598, the civil war continued unabated. In the years of relative peace that followed, the Protestants built churches in Saint-Martin, La Flotte, and Ars. Then came Henri IV's assassination in 1610 and Louis XIII's accession to the throne. Backed by Richelieu, he looked unfavourably on the military might of La Rochelle and the Protestants' hold on Ré. After a terrible battle at sea in September 1625, the Catholics again took over the island.

The construction of Fort de la Prée and the first citadel in Saint-Martin which had a garrison of 2,000 men took the island to 1627, the year in which terrifying rumours claimed that an English fleet was preparing to leave Portsmouth under the leadership of the Duke of Buckingham.

The siege of Saint-Martin and the royalist victory

At the end of the month of July, more than 60 English ships carrying almost 10,000 men entered the Pertuis Breton. The people of La Rochelle refused to join Buckingham who decided to capture Ré.

The initial attack, on Sablanceaux, was followed by a ceasefire during which Monsieur de Toiras and his men were able to seek refuge in the citadel in Saint-Martin and in Fort de la Pré. By 30th July, the entire island was under English control with the exception of these two strongholds. The attackers then instigated the long siege of Saint-Martin which was to last more than three months.

Overleaf: An aerial view of the salt-pans. For many years, especially in the 18th Century, salt was the island's main source of wealth.

Food quickly ran short and Toiras decided to inform the king of the situation and ask for assistance. To do so, he had to elude the English watch, a difficult task because they controlled all crossings between the island and the mainland. In the end, on 23rd August, three volunteers set off to swim across. One was washed away by the current; a second one was captured by the English. The third one arrived on the other side, fairly exhausted. Richelieu quickly prepared a victualling expedition which, miraculously, succeeded in avoiding the enemy and arrived in the citadel.

This provided only brief respite. Soon food was again in short supply and disease began to spread among the troops. Meanwhile, La Rochelle had fired on the French army and joined forces with English. In response, it suffered the longest siege in its history. Toiras, exhausted by the turn of events, sent one last desperate message to the king and envisaged surrender if no help was forthcoming. In the night of 7th October, a flotilla of 35 ships carrying men, food and munitions, succeeded in passing through the English lines again. The joy of those in the citadel contrasted sharply with the consternation expressed by the Duke of Buckingham. It was all the greater because winter was approaching and the condition of his troops was worsening.

A third and fourth flotilla landed at Fort de la Prée, despite heavy losses, on 17th and 30th October. Buckingham had had enough. He decided to launch one last decisive attack on the citadel. However, in the thick of battle, he received news of the arrival of royal troops from La Prée. It was too much for the Englishman who decided to lift the siege. The French pursued the enemy troops who re-embarked amid indescribable panic north of Loix, leaving behind huge numbers of corpses. The crisis was over. The English had failed, La Rochelle had lost its ally, and the Island of Ré returned to the French crown - not without some regrettable consequences for the Protestants.

An old windmill in Saint-Clément-des-Baleines.

The island's heyday

Once peace had returned, efforts were made under Louis XIII, Louis XIV and Vauban to provide Ré with protection against any future attacks. Fort de la Prée was modernised, redoubts were built, and coastal batteries were constructed. In 1696, they repulsed the Anglo-Dutch fleet. The original lighthouse was built at the western tip of the island. The citadel in Saint-Martin was rebuilt to a new layout and the entire town was encircled by walls. Finally, a royal garrison was stationed on the island.

As far as the economy was concerned, the recovery soon made itself felt, facilitated by the granting of privileges. The most important of these was Ré's status as a foreign country outside French excise boundaries. Very soon, the island's farms, wine-growing estates and salt-pans began to flourish (throughout the 18th Century more than 30,000 kegs of wine and almost 25,000 tonnes of salt were produced every year) and trade developed with the French coast and with Scandinavia, Santo Domingo and the East Indies.

The privileges granted to the islanders brought them a highly-developed social, community and political life with parish councils and general assemblies which sometimes went against the opinions of the island's governor who was the king's representative. New religious orders set up communities, assisting in the island's development and erecting many buildings including the superb Hôtel des Cadets Gentilshommes de la Marine in Saint-Martin which was constructed under the leadership of Father Ignatius.

It was a prosperous little country with a population of twenty thousand, a country that had finally regained its quiet serenity but which was soon to find itself whirled away in the torments of revolutionary France.

The French Revolution - hard times for Ré

With all the privileges granted to it, it was obvious that the island was going to suffer during the Revolution. The advantages were repealed one after the other, in particular the excise agreement making it a «foreign country». Civil disorder broke out. More especially, the uprising in Vendée made the supply of grain more and more unsure and the island was on the brink of famine. The Reign of Terror had its victims including the famous Gustave Dechezeaux who went to the scaffold in Rochefort on 17th January 1794. As to non-juring priests, they were imprisoned in the citadel in Saint-Martin. Those who survived captivity died later in Rochefort, in terrible agony.

The consequences of this social upheaval included the collapse of the economy and a general feeling of discontent aggravated by famine and the black market.

The 19th Century, good news and bad news

The Restoration of the monarchy brought new problems with the levying of taxes designed to improve the country's economic situation. It took time to calm things down.

The strong military presence continued until Napoleon's downfall but then declined. The numbers decreased steadily throughout the 19th Century. As far as trade was concerned,

Over the past few years, oyster farming has become one of the main sources of income for the island. In this photo, the oysters are being cleaned ready for sale.

wine and salt continued to be sold at reasonable prices and international trade regained some of its erstwhile vitality, even though it was in a period of decline. The real difficulties began in the late 19th Century. Between 1830 and 1860, major construction projects were launched. The wet dock was built in Saint-Martin, a steamship service was introduced between the island and La Rochelle, the first stages of a road network were created and the great lighthouse, the Phare des Baleines, was built in 1849.

In the second half of the century, however, two events suddenly took the wind out of the island's economic sails. Firstly, a law was passed regulating the salt trade and the ensuing authorisation to import foreign salt dealt a death blow to the salt-pans on Ré. Secondly, from 1875 onwards, a phylloxera epidemic destroyed most of the vineyards and it took years to work back up to average output.

It was obvious that the island had lost its strategic importance but it still had its magnificent citadel which was turned into a prison. In 1872, the supporters of the Commune who had been sentenced to deportation were imprisoned here for some time before being sent to New Caledonia. Dreyfus was held here and the hard labour camp continued to function until the Second World War.

Despite numerous efforts to improve life on the island, the economic decline caused an ever-increasing number of people to leave. The exodus was to continue until after the Second World War.

The two world wars

With the Great War, the island lost a few more of its population. After the Armistice, the population tried to revive the flagging economy by diversifying crops, developing the early vegetable market, and modernising wine production. The situation was just beginning to take an upturn when the Second World War broke out and the island was then occupied until 1945. It bristled with defensive constructions, none of which was ever used.

Ré since the 1950's - recovery, tourism and the bridge

Since the end of the war, the island seems to have changed a great deal. Although the salt-pans are, unfortuna-

The beautifully wild shoreline at the western tip of the Island of Ré. A flock of brent geese can be seen riding the waves.

tely, now disappearing, there are other more optimistic notes. Vineyards now cover almost 1,500 hectares and there is a high output of white wine, *pineau* (fortified wine) and cognac. Early vegetables and cereal crops are expanding. As the inshore fishing fleet declines, so there is an increase in the number of oysterbeds along the north coast in La Flotte and Loix.

The first effect of this recovery was to reverse the downturn in the population. It rose from just over 8,000 in 1950 to 11,388 in 1982. It is also obvious that the building of the bridge, which was officially opened in the summer of 1988, has greatly increased this figure now that La Rochelle is only ten minutes away from the island.

The most spectacular change, however, is undoubtedly the arrival and considerable expansion of the tourist industry. In 1980 the Blue Guide to Poitou-Charentes estimated the summer population of Ré to be an amazing 180,000, almost 18 times its usual figure! Nowadays, thanks to the building of the bridge, the number of summer visitors has increased still further, with the usual consequences as regards the development of tourist infrastructures, campsites and various amenities. The main problem, as always, is how to keep this development under control. History has shaped the island of Ré, the islanders, the architecture and the landscape, giving them all a wonderful balance that is as charming as it is «exotic». Everybody should bear this in mind so that two requirements can be reconciled - the need to open the island's doors to the outside world while ensuring that it retains its own personality and identity.

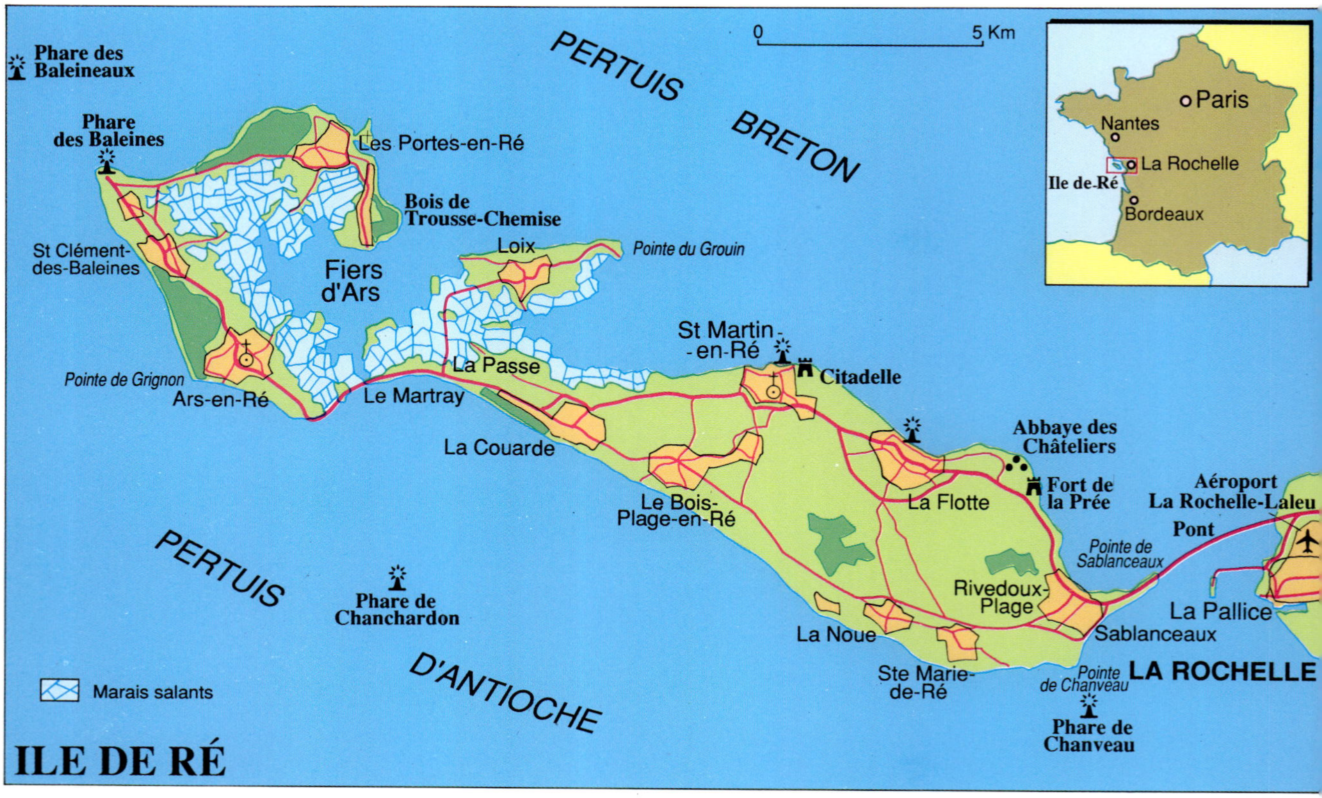

Carte : Patrick Mérienne

Front cover : The harbour in La Flotte-en-Ré.

Back cover : The old lighthouse (Phare des Baleines) at the westernmost tip of the island.

ISBN : 978-2-87901-232-2 - Editeur : 589.02.02.04.08 - N° d'impression : 46697B